TRUE Life

Colin Urquhart

Kingdom Faith Resources Ltd.
Roffey Place, Old Crawley Road,
HORSHAM West Sussex, RH12 4RU
Tel: 01293 851543 Fax: 01293 854610
E-mail: resources@kingdomfaith.com
www.kingdomfaith.com

First published in Great Britain in July 2001 by Kingdom Faith

Kingdom Faith Trust is a registered charity (no.278746)

ISBN 1-900409-28-3

Acknowledgements

My thanks to Hannah Shepherd for her help with editing the text; to Diane Garnham for typing the original manuscript; to David Stearns for typesetting this book and to Clarissa Musson for designing the cover. We all desire to give glory to God the Father for His *true life.*

Colin Urquhart July 2001

Contents

INTRODUCTION   7

THE CRUCIAL ACT   9

CRUCIFIED WITH CHRIST   13

YOUR PLACE IN CHRIST   21

WHAT YOU CAN DO IN CHRIST   39

YOUR PORTRAIT IN CHRIST   47

CONFESSING WHO YOU ARE IN CHRIST   55

THE TRUTH ABOUT YOUR PLACE IN CHRIST

There can be no greater truth for you to know and understand than your position in Christ. As a believer your relationship with the Father, and your walk of faith depends on this revelation.

It is sad that many people who are born again have little sense of their position in Christ, even though this is a key element of New Testament teaching. Ignorance of this essential truth results in many living in false condemnation and spiritual failure. Whereas, they could be full of confidence and thankfulness, for the wonderful privilege given to them the moment they committed their lives to Christ and were placed *'in Him'* by God the Father.

Those who have lived in the good of this place in Christ, testify to the way in which this truth has transformed their lives. They realise that this is the supreme work of God's grace; that He has taken hold of their lives and placed them *in Christ Jesus*, despite their sense of inadequacy and unworthiness.

No one could deserve to be in such a wonderful position, neither could they earn such a privilege. It is a gift from God to all who believe in Jesus Christ as Lord and Saviour.

THE CRUCIAL ACT

Before his conversion to Christ, the apostle Paul was an arch-enemy of the Christian Church. As Saul of Tarsus, he saw it as his God-given responsibility to persecute the early believers as heretics, and he even consented to their deaths. However, Paul's personal confrontation with Jesus on the road to Damascus radically altered his entire perception of Jesus and those who trusted in Him. He became a chief advocate of the faith he had tried to destroy. This happened because he came to understand his position in Christ, both on the cross and now in heaven. He learned to live daily *in Christ* and taught others to do so.

IT IS AN ACT OF GOD THE FATHER TO TAKE HOLD OF YOUR LIFE AND PUT YOU 'IN CHRIST'.

It is because of him that you are in Christ Jesus. (1 Cor 1:30)

**It is an act of God the Father to take hold of your life and put you *in Christ.* How can we understand what this means?

Take a small piece of paper and place it in your Bible. Now close the book. Imagine the Bible represents Christ, and you are the piece of paper. Your life is now *in Christ* in the same way the paper is in the book. The paper maintains its separate identity, it does not become part of the book itself, nevertheless, wherever the book goes the paper goes and wherever the paper goes the book goes!

This illustration helps us to understand our position in Christ, but cannot enable us to understand the profound truth that we take on the character of Christ. Every part of the life of Christ is given to those who are placed in Him. We shall understand more of this as we look at the Scriptures covering this subject.

First, though, you must be clear that it is God who has chosen to place you in Him. Just as you took the piece of paper and placed it in your Bible; it did not get there by its own effort or design, God has placed you in Christ. His purpose was that in living in Christ you should know that you are living in God and He in you.

Jesus said to His disciples: *"Abide in me and I in you" (John 15:4) NKJV.* Translated literally this means: *"Continue to live in me and I will continue to live in you".*

Many Christians understand the truth that Christ lives in them because they have received the precious gift of His Spirit, but they do not necessarily understand the complementary truth that they live in Christ Jesus, in God Himself. Paul told the Colossians:

> *For you died, and your life is now hidden with*
> *Christ in God. (Col 3:3)*

We will see what it means to say that we died with Christ so that we can know what it is to live *in Him.*

The apostle John says:

> *We know that we live in him and he in us, because*
> *he has given us of his Spirit. (1 John 4:13)*

Receiving the Holy Spirit, then, is evidence that you live in God and He lives in you. John goes on to say:

> *If anyone acknowledges that Jesus is the Son of God, God lives in*
> *him and he in God. (1 John 4:15)*

This is further evidence of this amazing truth. If anyone believes Jesus to be divine, God lives in them and they in Him. Notice that John does not say that the believer becomes God, or even part of God. The believer does not become divine. He states clearly that they live in God, and God lives in them!

THIS IS SOMETHING THAT HAS ALREADY TAKEN PLACE

So if you believe in Jesus Christ as your Lord and Saviour, are born again and have received the gift of God's Holy Spirit, then you can be sure that God has taken hold of your life and placed you *in Him*. This is something that has already taken place, whether you understand it or not. You do not have to *feel* in Christ to be in Christ; it is something God accomplished, even though you may have been completely unaware of it.

The implications of this truth are immense, for His life becomes your life and He has already blessed you in Christ with every spiritual blessing heaven has to give to God's children.

God performed this act at the very beginning of your Christian experience. You now need to discover the full implication of what He has already done, in order to live in the good of your position in Christ! You are not trying to make something happen: you realise this is an event that has already taken place, and you want to live in the good of your inheritance.

2

CRUCIFIED WITH CHRIST

Paul gives a potted version of his personal testimony in one verse:

I have been crucified with Christ and I no longer live, but Christ lives in me. The life I live in the body, I live by faith in the Son of God, who loved me and gave himself for me. (Gal 2:20)

We have seen that Paul told the Colossians that they had died, when clearly he was talking to people who were very much alive and living on planet earth! Now he speaks of his own crucifixion and the fact that he no longer lives. What does he mean?

Paul says: *"We are convinced that one died for all, therefore all died"* (2 Cor 5:14). All had sinned and fallen short of the glory of God. In order to restore us to relationship with Himself, it was necessary for God to send His Son to do what no other person had ever succeeded in doing. This was to live a sinless life of perfect obedience to His heavenly Father. **Jesus had to share our humanity completely, to be as weak as**

> JESUS HAD TO SHARE OUR HUMANITY COMPLETELY, TO BE AS WEAK AS WE ARE, BE TEMPTED IN EVERY WAY AS WE ARE, AND YET REMAIN SINLESS.

we are, to be tempted in every way as we are, and yet remain sinless:

For you know the grace of our Lord Jesus Christ, that though he was rich, yet for your sakes he became poor, so that you, through his poverty might become rich. (2 Cor 8:9)

Jesus became poor by leaving the glory of heaven to share in the poverty of our humanity. God's motive in this was to make us rich. This He has done by placing you *in Christ.* And yet not everyone lives in Christ today, as is obvious from the worldly lives lived by the vast majority of people.

Jesus did two things in becoming a man:

• He lived a life of perfect obedience.

• He offered His sinless life as a sacrifice for all those who have sinned.

It is commonly acknowledged among Christians that Jesus died for our sins. The Scriptures, however, teach us that He not only took our sins and iniquities on Himself, He also took sinners to the cross. In other words, all humanity! If one died, all mankind died.

Jesus was undoing the consequences of the sin of the first man, Adam. He sinned and all mankind shared in his fallen nature as a result. This means that everyone who is born into the world has a natural desire and inclination to sin. It is not long before the sweetest looking baby shows his or her naturally selfish instincts, the desire to do what self wants, rather than obey parental authority!

Because Jesus lived the sinless life of perfect obedience, all mankind can now be restored to relationship and fellowship with God. Jesus came as the second Adam to live the perfect life that Adam failed to live.

- **The sinless One has taken us as sinners to the cross and put us to death with Him!**

- **The perfect One has taken the imperfect to the cross so that now it is possible for us to be made perfect forever in God's sight. (See Heb 10:14)**

- **The obedient One has taken the disobedient to the cross that now we might live a new life of obedience to God.**

- **The successful One has crucified all failures with Him, so now we will be able to succeed in fulfilling God's plan and purpose for our lives.**

So Paul tells us that we have died with Christ, we were crucified with Him. Water baptism is really a funeral service, acknowledging that the old life has gone and that the new believer have been given a new life with Christ.

> *Or don't you know that all of us who were baptised into Christ Jesus were baptised into his death? We were therefore buried with him through baptism into death in order that just as Christ was raised from the dead through the glory of the Father, we too may live a new life. (Rom 6:3-4)*

Although Christ died for all, it is the act of personal faith in Him followed by water baptism that signifies that you have died and that your life is now hidden with Christ. Although Christ died for all, only those who through repentance and faith appropriate the work of the cross in their lives are raised to this new life in Him.

We cannot truly live in the good of our new life in Christ without first acknowledging what has been accomplished through our crucifixion with Christ.

> *For we know that our old self was crucified with him*
> *so that the body of sin might be done away with, that we should no*
> *longer be slaves to sin - because anyone who has died has been*
> *freed from sin. (Rom 6:6-7)*

The sin that bound and controlled us in the old life before we knew Christ, is now overcome because we live in Him, we live in the One who has overcome all sin. Faith in Him enables any believer to overcome all sin. You do not have to fight or revisit the sins of the past, for the sinner you were has now been put to death. You have become a new creation, living in Christ and by the person of the Holy Spirit, Christ lives in you:

> *Therefore, if anyone is in Christ, he is a new creation;*
> *the old has gone; the new has come! All this is from God, who*
> *reconciled us to himself through Christ and gave us the*
> *ministry of reconciliation. (2 Cor 5:17-18)*

Christ came and died for all; He took all sinful mankind to the cross. **Faith in what Jesus has done for you on the cross not only enables all your sins to be forgiven, but also for the power of sin in your life to be broken.** You no longer have to continue in the life of sin that was such an offence to God. He has completely forgiven and accepted you through faith in the blood of Jesus Christ and made it possible for you to live a righteous life.

Now you are a new creation. The old has gone, it's dead and buried, and the new has come.

Repentance and faith put you into agreement with God and enable you to be identified with Christ, crucified, risen from the dead and ascended victoriously to heaven. Repentance involves receiving forgiveness of sins and surrendering to the Lordship of Jesus Christ. It involves having a change of heart and mind, a complete change of direction for your life. Because you identify with Him on the cross, you are granted the privilege of sharing in His risen life and being seen by God as seated with Christ in heavenly places.

In your *old* life, you lived for yourself, walking in the ways of this world, the flesh and the devil. However once you have identified with the work of Jesus on the cross, you are *saved* from your former way of life. The old person you were, motivated by your sinful nature, has now died. You are a new creation, given a new heart, and a new nature with Christ living in you. You are now alive in Christ, a saint, one who is called and set apart by God to be His child.

REPENTANCE AND FAITH PUT YOU INTO AGREEMENT, AND IDENTIFY YOU WITH CHRIST.

Do you not know that your body is a temple of the Holy Spirit, who is in you, whom you have received from God? You are not your own; you were bought at a price. Therefore honour God with your body. (1 Cor 6:19-20)

Through the shedding of His blood, Jesus has paid the price for you, a sinner to be *redeemed*. Your sin once separated you from God and from fellowship with Him, but now you belong to Him.

This is the mercy of God. Instead of dealing with you as you deserve, God forgives you and makes you one with Him. He takes hold of you and places you in Christ. By putting your faith in the sacrificial work of Jesus you have become a son of God, and a co-heir with Christ.

> *You are all sons of God through faith in Christ Jesus, for all of you who were baptised into Christ have clothed yourselves with Christ. (Gal 3:26)*

> *So you are no longer a slave, but a son; and since you are a son, God has also made you an heir. (Gal 4:7)*

> *The Spirit himself testifies with our spirit that we are God's children. Now if we are children, then we are heirs - heirs of God and co-heirs with Christ. (Rom 8:16-17)*

Turning to Christ and putting your faith in Him means that:

- Jesus' blood cleanses you from all your former sins and from the punishment of God's condemnation that you deserved.

- Because you acknowledged you were one with Him on the cross, you are also made one with Him in His risen life. This is effected by God taking hold of your life and putting you in Christ - an act of sheer grace on His part.

- You are able to share fully in His life. Your old life is dead and buried; this is signified by your baptism. You are now a new creation in Christ, and with Christ living in you through the gift of the Holy Spirit.

- You are a son of God, a child of God, a co-heir with Christ. God is your Father who loves you and cares for you, He has placed you in His Son so you may enjoy the fullness of His life that He came to give you. Jesus said:

> *The thief [the devil] comes only to steal and kill and destroy; I have come that they may have life, and have it to the full. (John 10:10)*

3

YOUR PLACE IN CHRIST

Jesus told the disciples to remain in Him. **They were placed in Christ by God's gracious act, but they had the responsibility to continue to live out their lives in Him.**

And so it is for you and all believers today. Through His grace, God has placed you in Christ that you might live in Him. To enable you to continue in this, you need revelation of what it means to be in Christ. Paul helps us here. He sees that it is essential for Christians to recognise their position in Christ.

When writing to the Corinthians, he addresses them as, *"those sanctified in Christ Jesus and called to be holy" (1 Cor 1:2).* He addresses the Christians in Ephesus as *"the faithful in Christ Jesus" (Eph 1:1).* At Philippi they are called *"the saints in Christ Jesus" (Phil 1:1).* At Colosse Paul calls the believers *"the holy and faithful brothers in Christ" (Col 1:2).* When writing one of his earliest letters he addresses it *"To the church of the Thessalonians in God our Father and the Lord Jesus Christ" (1 Thess 1:1).*

So we can see that Paul regarded the whole church of born again believers as those living in Christ Jesus. This was not some special privilege accorded to the spiritually elite. It is a special privilege given to every born again believer!

If, therefore, you belong to Christ, you live in Him and He in you. Whatever the Scriptures say about being in Christ are therefore truths about you personally.

THIS ALLOWS THOSE WHO PUT THEIR FAITH IN HIM TO BE FULLY IDENTIFIED WITH HIM IN HIS GLORY.

The amazing truth is that Jesus came to share our humanity and identified completely with us in our need. This allows those who put their faith in Him to be fully identified with Him in His glory.

Put very simply, Jesus came to share your life so that now you may share in His life. This is the supernatural life of God that is much greater and more wonderful than simply living at the level of our humanity. Jesus came into our situation on earth so that by living in Him, we may live the same life He lived here on earth.

If this seems extraordinary, it is no more than Jesus promised the disciples:

> *I tell you the truth, anyone who has faith in me will do what I have been doing. He will do even greater things than these because I am going to be with the Father. (John 14:12)*

We are as He is in the world; what an amazing truth. This is not how most Christians see themselves. They tend to look at themselves and concentrate on their own weakness and failure and their inability to overcome temptation and sin. They are more aware of their feelings of frustration and doubt than of their position in Christ.

Paul was a great encourager. When writing his first letter to the Corinthians he was addressing a situation where chaos and disorder reigned. There was just about every conceivable problem in the church there; gross immorality that went uncorrected, divisions, jealousies and party factions. There were many disputes about the exercise of spiritual gifts. There were even some drunkenness when they met together.

Instead of immediately addressing these issues, Paul began the letter by reminding them of the truth of who they were in Christ. He addresses them as those *sanctified in Christ Jesus*. This means that God has already made them a holy people, called them and set them apart to be His own. He has placed them in His holy Son and they live in Him.

So what did they think they were doing acting in such ungodly ways? This is his message later in the letter. What he says at first is that they are sanctified in Christ and called to be holy; but they are also called to live according to the position they have been given by God. However before bringing them the correction they need, Paul encourages them with some wonderful truths about their position in Christ.

I always thank God for you because of his grace given
you in Christ Jesus. (1 Cor 1:4)

Even though they were experiencing great problems, they were still in Christ. They were the recipients of His grace: He had chosen to give them everything although they deserved nothing. Christ had been pleased to accept them as His own. Paul is happy to recognise this by always thanking God for them, not thinking badly of them!

For in him you have been enriched in every way - in all your speaking and in all your knowledge. (1 Cor 1:5)

GOD WANTS YOU TO KNOW THE TRUTH OF YOUR POSITION IN HIM, AND FOR YOUR THOUGHTS, WORDS, AND ACTIONS TO BE CONSISTENT WITH THE REVELATION OF THIS POSITION.

Remember, what is true of those believers in Christ is also true of you. Because you are in Him, you have been enriched in every way! Paul reinforces this truth by addressing this letter, not only to the Christians in Corinth, but to *"all those everywhere who call on the name of the Lord Jesus Christ"*. That is a fine description of you as a believer in Him.

So, He has enriched you in every way. The Corinthians were rich in their speech and knowledge, but they didn't act accordingly. **God wants you to know the truth of your position in Him, and for your thoughts, words, and actions to be consistent with the revelation of this position.**

What does it mean to be enriched in every way? Paul says:

Therefore you do not lack any spiritual gift as you eagerly wait for our Lord Jesus Christ to be revealed. He will keep you strong to the end, so that you will be blameless on the day of our Lord Jesus Christ. (1 Cor 1:7-8)

You do not lack any spiritual gift! Whatever gift you need is available to you - how wonderful! You must, however, take hold of these gifts and use them in the right way; not in a chaotic way as was the case in Corinth at that time.

It is because of him that you are in Christ Jesus, who has become for us wisdom from God - that is, our righteousness, holiness and redemption. (1 Cor 1:30)

Because you are in Him, Jesus is now your *wisdom from God.* This means He has done for you what you could never do for yourself.

YOU DO NOT LACK ANY SPIRITUAL GIFT!

- **He is your righteousness.** What does this mean? It means that God does not look upon you as being apart from Christ, but actually in Him. His righteousness becomes your righteousness. He sees you as He sees Jesus. He treats you as He treats Jesus. He relates to you as He relates to Jesus, because of your position in Him.

- **He is your holiness.** You cannot make yourself holy before the Holy God. The blood of Jesus has washed you clean from all your sins; but your position in Christ does even more than that. God regards you as holy because you are in His holy Son; and He has put His Holy Spirit in you to enable you to live a holy life.

- **He is your redemption.** He has paid the price, with the sacrifice of His life that enables you to belong to God forever. You are not condemned and eternally separated from God, as you deserve because of your sin, but: *"The punishment that brought us peace was upon him" (Isaiah 53:5).*

When writing to the Ephesians, Paul writes of the same truths in a different way. He tells his readers:

Praise be to the God and Father of our Lord Jesus Christ, who has blessed us in the heavenly realms with every spiritual blessing in Christ. (Eph 1:3)

You have been blessed with every spiritual blessing in Christ. The tense of the word is important. Paul does not say that this is what God wants to do. God has already done this. It is an accomplished fact: **He HAS blessed you with EVERY spiritual blessing in Christ.** Not some of the blessings of Christ, but every blessing that is His in heaven is already given to you here on earth! Isn't that amazing?

Why should He have done such a thing? The next verse tells us:

For he chose us in him before the creation of the world to be holy and blameless in his sight. (Eph 1:4)

Even before He created the world, God decided that all those in Christ would be enriched in every way, that they would be given every spiritual blessing in Christ. This has nothing to do with your performance as a Christian. God chose to do this before you became a believer, even before you existed. It is a complete work of His grace; what He has chosen to give you, not what you have earned or deserved.

Why should He have placed YOU in Christ? So that you would be holy and blameless in His sight now and for all eternity. Yet you did absolutely nothing to achieve this. All you did was to ask Jesus

to forgive your sins and surrendered your life
to Him that He might be your Lord.

When we surrender we sometimes think we
are going to lose out. With God it is the very
opposite. **Surrendering to Him enables us to
share the fullness of life in Christ.** We gain
infinitely more than we could ever give away.

SURRENDERING
TO HIM ENABLES US
TO SHARE THE
FULLNESS OF LIFE
IN CHRIST.

It is in love that He chose to adopt us as His sons:

> *In love he predestined us to be adopted as his sons through Jesus
> Christ, in accordance with his pleasure and will. (Eph 1:5)*

It wasn't your idea, but His! He chose to adopt you as His child.
He chose to put you into Christ because He wanted you to live
with Him eternally. As Jesus said:

> *You did not choose me, but I chose you and appointed you
> to go and bear fruit - fruit that will last. Then the Father will give
> you whatever you ask in my name. (John 15:16)*

God has not chosen to put you into Christ that you might simply
exist in Him; but to enable you to live a fruitful life for Him. He
has a plan and purpose for your life. You are a small part of God's
master plan:

> *"… to bring all things in heaven and on earth together under
> one head, even Christ. In him we were also chosen, having been
> predestined according to the plan of him who works out everything
> in conformity with the purpose of his will. (Eph 1:10-11)*

From these verses you see that God is in complete control, and He will ensure that everything works out in the way He has planned. He knows the end from the beginning.

The extraordinary truth is that He has made you a part of that plan. In every successive generation, He has those who live in Christ and are called to carry forward His purpose, preparing the way for Christ to come again, not as the Suffering Servant, but as the Triumphant King. All that do not acknowledge His Lordship will then be judged, whereas all who live in Him will enter into the fullness of their inheritance in Christ. They will rule and reign with Him for all eternity, that includes you! Meanwhile, you have to live out Jesus' life in *this present evil age.* However, you do not do that alone; you live out your life *in Christ!* He is the one who has already overcome. And so Paul affirms:

> But thanks be to God, who always leads us in triumphal
> procession in Christ and through us spreads everywhere the
> fragrance of the knowledge of him. (2 Cor 2:14)

God ALWAYS leads us in triumph in Christ! Some Christians do not like talk of triumph. However, God loves such faith, believing what He says in His Word, that He will ALWAYS lead us triumphantly in Christ!

Clearly, there can be no failure, no sin, and no fear in Christ. **When we speak negatively we are not, at that point, allowing God to lead us according to our position in Christ.** At such times God does not wash His hands of us, neither does He throw us out of Christ as miserable failures. He has placed us in Christ and now wants to teach us how to live in Him. When we do, we are conscious of God leading us in His triumphal procession.

Failure is an indication that we do not yet fully trust Him. There are occasions when we do not follow Him, when we are not conscious of our position in Christ. We therefore fail to avail ourselves of the full riches of our inheritance in Him. When we do fail though, He is ready to forgive us and restore us in our walk in Christ.

WHEN WE SPEAK NEGATIVELY WE ARE NOT, AT THAT POINT, ALLOWING GOD TO LEAD US ACCORDING TO OUR POSITION IN CHRIST.

This is our biggest dilemma. So often there seems an enormous gap between our position in Christ and our actual performance, what we do in our everyday lives. I call this the credibility gap.

YOUR POSITION IN CHRIST

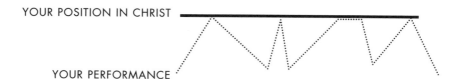

YOUR PERFORMANCE

However, the best truth you will ever receive is this:

Your performance does not affect your position in Christ. Your position is a work of God's grace in response to your faith and has nothing to do with your performance. His intention is that, by His grace, you will continue to live in Him, and not live as if you are not in Him.

Although your position has nothing to do with your performance, this does not give you the right to abuse God's grace by not caring about your performance. No, God wants your performance to model your position. These are the times when He is truly glorified in your life. It grieves Him when you are careless about the way you live. It pleases Him when you believe that you are who He says you are in Christ. It pleases Him when you believe you have what He says you have because you are in Christ. It pleases Him to see you speaking and living out your life in Him, doing what He says you are able to do because you are in Christ.

But because of his great love for us, God, who is rich in mercy,
made us alive with Christ even when we were dead in transgressions
- it is by grace you have been saved.(Eph 2:4-5)

The entire work is a matter of God's grace. However, the revelation Paul gives us is even more wonderful. Because we are in Christ, God sees us already seated with Him in heavenly places:

And God raised us up with Christ and seated us with him
in the heavenly realms in Christ Jesus, in order that in the
coming ages he might show the incomparable riches of his grace,
expressed in his kindness to us in Christ Jesus. (Eph 2:6-7)

Notice again that Paul uses the past tense. God raised us up with Christ and *has already* seated us with Him in heavenly places! How can this be when we are clearly still here on earth?

Because He dwells in eternity, God can see the end from the beginning. He can describe the future prophetically in Scripture with such accuracy because He already sees it. In eternity it is possible to see the past, the present and the future because God is outside the restrictions of time.

Because He knows the end from the beginning, He sees you already seated in heavenly places. Your citizenship is in heaven; this is where you belong! And this is why Jesus teaches us to pray: *"May your Kingdom come; may your will be done on earth as it is in heaven"*.

Paul could never escape the lavish nature of God's grace. He regarded himself as the chief of sinners for persecuting the Church. That he should deserve damnation and yet be seated in heavenly places in Christ, was the most incredible demonstration of God's grace. All who know Jesus personally say *'Amen'* to that!

> *For it is by grace you have been saved, through faith - and this is not from yourselves, it is the gift of God - not by works, so that no one can boast. (Eph 2:8-9)*

Because all this is the work of God's grace we cannot claim any credit ourselves. However, although we have the assurance of an eternal inheritance, we are not free to do what we like! We are not our own; we have been bought at a price. We are placed in Christ Jesus for God's plan and purpose for our lives to be fulfilled.

> *For we are God's workmanship, created in Christ Jesus to do good works, which God prepared in advance for us to do. (Eph 2:10)*

He chose not only to put you into Christ, but He also chose the works you are to perform in Christ - good works. These are not the things of the flesh that spring from what you want to do, but the things that come from what the Spirit leads you to do: the works the Holy Spirit does in and through you. The works you could only do because you live in Christ and He in you.

HE WILL ENABLE THE FULFILMENT OF GOD'S PLAN FOR YOUR LIFE.

They are the works you will do as a part of His body here on earth, the body through which God has chosen to fulfil His purpose in creation!

Together with other believers you are being built *"to become a dwelling in which God lives by his Spirit" (Eph 2:22)*. So the Holy Spirit lives in you personally; He lives also in the Body of Christ of which you are a member. **He will enable the fulfilment of God's plan for your life, as an individual part of His purpose for His Body, through which He will bring about His will for the whole of creation.**

This helps you to realise that you are part of something God has planned that is much bigger than the daily circumstances of your life that probably preoccupy you. If God could have fulfilled everything He had planned without you, then He would not have included you. You may feel very insignificant in yourself; yet to God you have an important and significant part to play in what He has determined to do. **Nobody living in Christ Jesus could be insignificant to Him.**

He knows your thoughts, your words, your heart attitudes, your actions and even how many hairs are on your head! So He must want to be involved in the details of your life. There is no point in trying to hide from Him because He knows all about you; it is pointless to try and fool Him. There is no point in acting, putting on a front or trying to deceive Him. He sees through every performance. He is the truth and He wants you to be real with Him.

So in seeing yourself in Christ you are not being unreal, but you are seeing yourself as He truly sees you:

> *In him and through faith in him we may approach God with freedom and confidence. (Eph 3:12)*

And this is what He wants, for you to approach Him with freedom and confidence. You can be as open and honest with Him as you like. You can pour out your heart to Him, and He will pour out His heart to you.

However, He will want you to see that in the natural you may struggle, feel perplexed and even frustrated because you are battling with so many trying circumstances; yet the spiritual truth is that you are in Christ and He in you. **You are therefore able to overcome, no matter what the circumstances. Those trying situations can never take you outside of His wonderful love!**

> *And I pray that you, being rooted and established in love, may have power, together with all the saints, to grasp how wide and long and high and deep is the love of Christ, and to know this love that surpasses knowledge - that you may be filled to the measure of all the fullness of God. (Eph 3:17-19)*

Notice Paul is addressing all saints here, all who are in Christ and belong to Him. He wants all the saints to know how exclusive God's love is and that nothing in the whole of creation can separate them from that love.

> *For I am convinced that neither death nor life, neither angels nor demons, neither the present nor the future, nor any powers, neither height nor depth, nor anything else in all creation, will be able to separate us from the love of God that is in Christ Jesus our Lord. (Rom 8:38-39)*

Paul knew this from his own experience. He could be open and honest about the trying circumstances that constantly afflicted him, yet he never lost the sense of victory that he knew was his because he was in Christ. None of these trying situations could separate him from the love of God in Christ, in which he lived!

> *We are hard pressed on every side, but not crushed; perplexed, but not in despair; persecuted, but not abandoned; struck down, but not destroyed. (2 Cor 4:8-9)*

Being a man of faith, he goes on to say:

> *It is written: "I believed; therefore I have spoken." With that same spirit of faith we also believe and therefore speak. (2 Cor 4:13)*

He doesn't speak fear, failure and despondency over his life. He speaks the will and purpose of God over his life, knowing the inheritance that is his in Christ. He believes that he is in Christ and speaks accordingly. He appreciates that to live the gospel in an unbelieving world is going to prove costly, but He says:

*"We do not lose heart", he says ... For our light and
momentary troubles are achieving for us an eternal glory
that far outweighs them all. (2 Cor 4:16-17)*

We are to fix our eyes on what is unseen, our position in Christ, and how His grace is sufficient for us, no matter what the situation. No difficulty, no attack, no opposition can take you out of Christ where God has placed you! Jesus taught Paul:

*"My grace is sufficient for you, for my power is made
perfect in weakness." Therefore I will boast all the more
gladly about my weaknesses, so that Christ's power
may rest on me. (2 Cor 12:9)*

This doesn't mean that Paul went around speaking negatively about himself, complaining about the cost he was facing for obeying his call from Jesus, quite the opposite.

He knew that because he was loved and accepted perfectly in Christ, nothing could separate him from God's love in Christ and his personal weakness didn't matter. All of God's resources were available to him. He knew, *"when I am weak, then I am strong"*. *(2 Cor 12:10)*

Most Christians are only too aware of their weakness, but they condemn themselves to failure because, unlike Paul, they do not recognise the strength they have in Christ. They walk around feeling sorry for themselves, often eliciting pity from others, feeling that there is no way out of their problems. They fail to recognise that this weakness doesn't matter because they live in the One who cannot fail, cannot be overcome and from whose love they cannot be separated!

This is true faith. Paul does not live in denial. He does not pretend the trying circumstances or the problems that confront him do not exist, but he knows that these problems will never have the last word. After all *"God chose the weak things of the world to shame the strong" (1 Cor 1:27).*

In saying that he will boast of the things that show his weakness *(2 Cor 12:9)*, Paul is not being negative, instead he is giving glory to God. **Everything God does in or through us is a work of His grace, effected by His Holy Spirit.**

All this should encourage us. For we see it really does not matter how weak we feel in ourselves, so long as we know who we are in Christ. We will not walk around thinking or saying: "I'm no good, I'm just a useless failure. God couldn't do anything mighty in me or through me. I always get things wrong. I am the one who always seems to miss out on the blessings!"

Paul would never think like that. His attitude would be: "Praise God that by His grace I am in Christ Jesus. His life is my life. In myself I am weak, but that doesn't matter. In Him I am strong. And His grace is sufficient for me. His power is revealed in me despite my weakness. Nothing can separate me from His love and He has already blessed me with every spiritual blessing in Christ."

What a contrast! And this is how you should see yourself. Being in Christ, you have the same life, the same grace and the same blessings that were available to Paul and the other apostles. It is for this reason that Paul says:

> *His divine power has given us everything we need for life and godliness through our knowledge of him who called us by his own glory and goodness. Through these he has given us his very great and precious promises, so that through them you may participate in the divine nature and escape the corruption in the world caused by evil desires. (2 Pet 1:3-4)*

The *"very great and precious promises"* relate to all that God has done for us through Christ and all that He says is yours because you live in Him. How can we speak of ourselves in failure and defeat if we truly believe we *"participate in the divine nature"*, that we live in Christ who can know no defeat and can never be overcome? When Paul speaks of the conflict we know so well; wanting to do what is right, but ending up doing the opposite, he asks:

> *What a wretched man I am! Who will rescue me from this body of death? Thanks be to God - through Jesus Christ our Lord! (Rom 7:24-25)*

God gives us the victory through Jesus Christ, in whom we live. Yes, in my weakness I am always prone to failure; but in Christ there is no limit to what God can and will accomplish in and through me!

This is the wonderful good news of the gospel. It is not God's purpose to make you stronger; He wants you to remain weak in yourself so that you will be strong in your faith. So that you will not trust in yourself but in your position in Christ; in who you are in Him and what you are able to do through faith in Him. So Paul says, "*The only thing that counts is faith expressing itself in love*" *(Gal 5:6)*.

Trusting in yourself is of no value whatsoever. This is in line with what Jesus said, "*Apart from me you can do nothing*" *(John 15:5)*.

Anything you do apart from Christ is therefore worth absolutely nothing. The only thing of value to God in your life is what you do in Christ and through His Spirit working in and through you. So Jesus teaches us:

> *Remain in me, and I will remain in you. No branch*
> *can bear fruit by itself; it must remain in the vine. Neither can*
> *you bear fruit unless you remain in me. (John 15:4)*

You are a branch of the true vine of Jesus Christ, grafted in by the Father Himself when you were born again; so you live in Christ. The sap of His Spirit will flow through your branch causing you to be fruitful as you live, abide, and remain in Him! Apart from Him you can do nothing, but by living in Him you can bear much fruit for the glory of the Father.

4

WHAT YOU CAN DO IN CHRIST

We have seen that: *"In him and through faith in him we may approach God with freedom and confidence" (Eph 3:12).* We do not have to creep into His presence as if this is not where we rightly belong. We are totally accepted in Christ; we can come right into the Holy of Holies, the very presence of God, through the blood of Jesus. The blood has cleansed us from our unworthiness and made us worthy in His sight.

We are in Christ and have the privilege of praying in His name, and we can be assured that *"my Father will give you whatever you ask in my name" (John 16:23).* **This is to be our expectation; that we can ask for whatever Jesus would ask for because we are in Him.** We can believe what He would believe, look at the circumstances, as He would view them - because we live in Him.

We know that nothing can separate us from the love of God that is in Christ Jesus. We know that in Him we have been enriched in every way.

> *There is but one Lord, Jesus Christ, through whom all things came and through whom we live. (1 Cor 8:6)*

We know also that God *"always leads us in triumphal procession in Christ"* *(2 Cor 2:14)*.

We have seen that *"we are weak in him, yet by God's power we will live with him to serve you"* *(2 Cor 13:4)*.

There are still other wonderful truths for us to take hold of in Christ: *You have been given fullness in Christ, who is the head over every power and authority (Col 2:10)*. You live in the One who is head over every power and authority. *"Having disarmed the powers and authorities, he made a public spectacle of them, triumphing over them by the cross" (Col 2:15)*. Therefore you do not have to live in fear of these powers and authorities. Instead you continue to live by faith in the One who has overcome and reigns victorious.

So then, just as you received Christ Jesus as Lord, continue to live in him, rooted and built up in him, strengthened in the faith as you were taught, and overflowing with thankfulness. (Col 2:6-7)

These are two very rich verses from which we can understand a number of significant truths.

- Paul is addressing all who have received Christ Jesus as Lord. So if you are a Christian, then these words are addressed to you.

- You have been placed in Christ so you are to continue to live in Him; to abide or remain in Him.

- You have been rooted in Him. As He is the Word of God, this means you are rooted in His Word, through which you have assurance that you are in Christ. You have the revelation of your inheritance in Him. He is the source of your life in the Spirit.

- The truth of who you are in Christ is at the heart of your faith and your daily Christian walk. The more you live in the revelation of who you are in Christ, the more you will be built up as a believer.

- To be rooted in Him is to be rooted in His love; to be built up in Him is to be built up in His love. The result is that you will be strengthened in your faith; *faith working through love.* This is the faith you are taught in God's Word: to live according to your position in Christ, laying hold of the inheritance you have in Him.

- As a result, you will overflow with thankfulness. For you know that your weakness does not matter as you have His life and strength as your inheritance in Christ. You will be thankful for His grace by which you have been given fullness of life in Christ. You will also be thankful that nothing can separate you from His love in Christ and that your faith in Him will enable you to overcome, no matter what the circumstances.

No wonder Paul says:

> *Since, then, you have been raised with Christ, set your heart on things above, where Christ is seated at the right hand of God. (Col 3:1)*

He is the One in whom you live!

Set your minds on things above, not on earthly things. For you died, and your life is now hidden with Christ in God. (Col 3:2-3)

It is not that Paul is living in a fantasy world; far from it. He has learned that to have victory on earth, you need to know who you are in heaven; one who is reigning in Christ Jesus. You have supernatural resources that enable you to overcome the natural weaknesses and temptations to which you are subjected on earth.

You can see yourself as weak and useless because you view yourself through your natural thoughts and emotions. Or you can see yourself as an overcomer because you are in Christ, the One who reigns supreme over all.

You will not live a life of victory by being double-minded, fluctuating from one opinion of who you are to another. *"He who doubts is a double-minded man, unstable in all he does"* (James 1:8). Such a man *"should not think he will receive anything from the Lord".* (James 1:7)

So you must make the decision once and for all, and not go back on that decision. Are you in Christ or not? If you are in Him because you are a Christian, then all we have seen about inheritance in Christ is true of you. **You make the decision, then, to see yourself in Christ, to think of yourself in Christ, possessing all that you have in Christ.** You agree not to think of yourself as outside of Him or separated from His love, but living in Him, rooted and built up in Him, possessing everything you need for life and godliness.

You believe, therefore, that you are who God says you are in Christ. You have what He says you have in Christ. You are able to do what He says you can do because you are in Christ.

You decide that you will not be seduced away from the truth by negative thoughts or feelings about yourself. You are weak, but you are not a failure, for there are no failures in Christ! You will not allow the enemy to persecute you with taunts that you cannot be in Christ because your performance seems so far removed from your position.

Blessed is the man who perseveres under trial, because when he has stood the test, he will receive the crown of life that God has promised to those who love him. (James 1:12)

No, you will hold fast to the truth of who God says you are, having His wisdom, knowledge and understanding that are far greater than your own. You do not live a life of disagreement with Him because you think you know better than He does, but you live the life of agreement He has called you to. You are prepared to humble yourself before the revelation of His Word, knowing that as He reveals the truth to you it is able to set you free from all false perceptions of yourself.

What will be the outworking of this faith?

Be joyful always; pray continually; give thanks in all circumstances, for this is God's will for you in Christ Jesus. (1 Thes 5:16-18)

Where have you been placed? In Christ Jesus! Where do you live? In Christ Jesus! What is His will for you in Him? That you are a joyful, prayerful, thankful person! That sounds very positive!
What is more, you will be able to give thanks in all circumstances because you know that no matter what your situation, you are in Christ the overcomer and nothing in all creation can separate you from God's love. **So the circumstances will not rule over you; in Christ you will prevail over the circumstances.**

THE CIRCUMSTANCES WILL NOT RULE OVER YOU; IN CHRIST YOU WILL PREVAIL OVER THE CIRCUMSTANCES.

This is faith in action. Can you see yourself as such a person? This is how God already sees you, being led in His triumphal procession in Christ - always!

Paul writes to Philemon:

I pray that you may be active in sharing your faith, so that you will have a full understanding of every good thing we have in Christ. (Philemon 6)

You will find that the more you talk to others about your position in Christ, the more the truth will grip your heart and life, enabling you to live in the good of it! This has certainly been my experience. I have taught these truths over many years to churches, Bible school students, pastors and leaders - every time I do so I am left in wonder of this amazing revelation.

So, instead of talking about the no good failure you have often seen yourself to be, talk of yourself as God sees you. Not in pride, of course, but with thankfulness for the amazing work of His grace. If there is no one else to listen, speak these truths to yourself over and over again.

In a ministry such as mine there are immense pressures. Like anyone else I can be confronted at times by situations that are exceedingly testing. I have learned at such times to speak out words of truth of who I am in Christ. Within a few minutes I can feel completely different, because instead of seeing the problems through natural eyes and feelings, I begin to see things from God's perspective - in Christ! I see things as He sees them, conscious that

I have fullness of life in Him. If I trust Him He will surely lead me through these difficulties in triumph - just as He has promised.

What a wonderful, faithful God! And how great His grace that He should take totally unworthy people such as you and me, and place us in Christ. That we might live in Him, co-heirs with Him of all that God has to give, already seated in Christ with every spiritual blessing in heavenly places!

5

YOUR PORTRAIT IN CHRIST

You know who you are in the natural, and every time you look in the mirror you see your natural appearance. It is good however to look into God's Word and see who you are in the Spirit. From all the revelation given in the New Testament, you can build a portrait of who you are in Christ. This is how God sees you in Him.

You are called and chosen by God
This is a work of His grace, in accordance with His own pleasure and will. He chose you because He wanted to choose you!

You have been crucified with Christ
When He went to the cross He took you, the sinner, with Him. He has put you to death to make you the new creation you are now.

So you have died
You died with Christ. So don't try to resurrect the old life. Don't go delving into the past that is dead and buried.

You have new life
You have been raised to new life with Him, through faith. His life has become your life.

You have a rich inheritance

You have been born again into *a living hope* and have been given *an inheritance that can never perish, spoil or fade.* You can be confident of your eternal destiny *in Him.*

You are set free

On the cross Jesus did everything necessary to free you from every bondage. He has set you free from sin and guilt, continual failure and a sense of weakness; from the oppressive work of the enemy, from sickness, grief and mental anguish. *It is for freedom Christ has set you free!*

You are made one with God

You have been made righteous, put in right relationship with God your Father through all Jesus has done for you. You have now been made one with Him, through the atoning work of His blood. Now you can live in agreement with Him.

You are made Holy

God sees you set apart for His purposes. You could never acquire a holiness of your own. Jesus' holiness becomes your holiness because you are in Him.

You are no longer under religious law

Jesus died to save you from the curse of the law - trying to please God through obedience to some religious code or system. Now His Spirit, living in you, can work in you true and loving obedience to Him.

Jesus intercedes for you

Jesus has entered heaven and appears before God for you.

His blood stands between God and the judgment you deserve for your sin. He speaks to the Father in your defence and you have direct access to the Father through Him.

You live in Christ Jesus

God put you in Him and has enriched you in every way. He has already blessed you with every heavenly blessing *in Him*.

You live by faith

By faith you appropriate all that God has done for you in Christ and all He has given you through Him! Through this faith, God has given you eternal life and made it possible for you to do the same things as Jesus. You participate in His divine nature and have been given His very great and precious promises. Everything is possible for you because you believe in Jesus.

God lives in you by His Spirit

He has set His seal of ownership on you by giving you His Holy Spirit. He is the Spirit of Truth who will guide you into all the truth, including the revelation of who you are in Christ - enabling you to live in this position. You are now able to love others with the same love with which He has loved you. Both the Father and Son have come to make their home within you.

You live in God's grace

By His grace God placed you in Christ, and by His grace you can live in Him daily. He has saved you by grace, lavished His grace on you so that in all things, at all times, having all that you need, you will abound in every good work. From the fullness of His grace, you are able to receive one blessing after another.

You are fruitful in Christ

By living, remaining, abiding in Christ as a branch of the True Vine, you bear much fruit for the Father's glory. Apart from Him you can do nothing. You not only receive His life, but that life can flow out of you like rivers of living water. You can serve, bless, encourage and give to others the life He has given to you.

You abide in His love

Jesus has demonstrated the extent of His love for you by dying for you, by taking you to live in Himself, and by sending His own Spirit to live in you. Nothing in all creation can now separate you from the love of God that is in Christ Jesus. You live, abide, remain in that love.

You are a son of God

Sons have the first right of inheritance and you are a co-heir with Christ; you share in the inheritance He has been given by the heavenly Father. As a son of God you belong to the Father and He cares for you and watches over you in His divine love.

Now you are able to obey God

Obedience is the outworking of your love for God. You are able to love because He has first loved you. This life of loving obedience to His Word, and therefore His will, will cause His joy to be in you and your joy to be full.

Now you walk in the light

Because you live in Christ you are to have nothing more to do with darkness. You are a child of the light, called to walk in the light of God's truth. His light is to shine out of you so that others may see your good works and give glory to your Father in heaven.

You act 'in His Name'

You can pray, speak and act in the name of Jesus. Whatever you do you are to do with all your heart, as working for the Lord. You are to do everything in His name, giving thanks to the Father through Him. This is God's will for you in Christ Jesus!

You are a man or woman of the Word

Because you live *in Christ Jesus*, you live in the Word of God. His words are to live in you, so that you are a doer and not a hearer only! God's Word tells you who you are in Christ, and what you are able to do because you are in Him. You can test all your thoughts, feelings and actions against God's Word to know if they are really in line with God's will.

You are 'weak in Him'

In your natural life, the flesh, you will always be weak, but you know that weakness can be your greatest strength, for God says: *"My grace is sufficient for you; my power is made perfect in your weakness."* So, like Paul, when you are weak, then you are strong! Weak in yourself, strong in Him!

Jesus has given you victory

You are strong in His mighty power. The Spirit within you has even overcome death! Because you are born of God, you have overcome the world, and He who is in you, the Holy Spirit, is greater than he who is in the world, the prince of darkness. So God always leads you in triumphal procession in Christ. By submitting yourself to God and resisting the devil, he will flee from you.

You are a member of Christ's body

Although you have a personal relationship with Christ, He calls you also to love and be at one with others who are in Him. You are a living stone built together with them into a holy temple - His people in the world, a holy nation belonging to God.

God will answer your prayer

You are to pray with faith, believing the words of promise God has given you, that if you ask anything in the name of Jesus, He will give it to you. The Holy Spirit is to direct you when praying, for He will reveal God's purpose to you by guiding you into the truth of His Word. Praying with faith means you *know* what the outcome of the prayer will be when you ask. Jesus said that you are to believe you have received whatever you ask in prayer. And He promises that all who ask receive.

You are able to draw near to God

When you pray you can approach God with freedom and confidence. You come into the Holy of holies with a thankful heart and in full assurance of faith. You come to the throne of grace where you will find mercy and grace to help you in your time of need. Draw near to Him and He will draw near to you!

You are a covenant child of God

God has made you part of the New Covenant, sealed with Jesus' blood. He will always remain faithful to you and will fulfil His words of promise to you. You are to be faithful to Him in fulfilling what He asks of you!

His promises are for you

God has given you His very great and precious promises by

which you are able to share in His life. He promises to forgive you when you confess your sins to Him. He will keep you from being ineffective and unproductive in your faith, and He graciously gives you all things in Christ. He will be with you always.

He meets your every need

God will meet every need of yours according to His riches in glory in Christ Jesus. As you seek first the Kingdom of God and His righteousness, everything else will be added to you. However, you will reap what you sow. So the measure you give will determine the measure you receive, although He gives good measure, pressed down, shaken together and running over!

Your future hope is in Jesus

He has given you eternal life and promises that you will not be condemned because you have already passed from death to life! You will be presented in His sight holy, without blemish and free from accusation.

You are part of His eternal Kingdom

God has made you a part of His eternal Kingdom. He has delivered you from the dominion of darkness and brought you into the Kingdom of the Son He loves. That Kingdom within you is like a seed that needs to grow, develop and become fruitful. You have your inheritance in His Kingdom, the Kingdom purposed for you before the creation of the world. The time will come when you will shine like the sun in the Kingdom of your Father when you appear with Him in glory in your resurrection body. When you see Him as He is, you will be like Him!

6

CONFESSING WHO YOU
ARE IN CHRIST

The Bible is very clear that the words we speak are of the utmost importance. Jesus pointed out that *"from the overflow of the heart the mouth speaks" (Matt 12:34)*. **Our words are an indication of what we believe in our hearts.** Not just the words we speak when we pray, but in every conversation. There is no point in saying we believe certain things when addressing God, while our other conversations make it clear that we do not believe those things, or at least are full of doubts concerning them!

> *For out of the overflow of the heart the mouth speaks.*
> *The good man brings good things out of the good stored up*
> *in him, and the evil man brings evil things out of the*
> *evil stored up in him. (Matt 12:34-35)*

The tongue gives away what is truly happening in our hearts. One of the most awesome things Jesus said is on this very subject:

> *But I tell you that man will have to give account on the day*
> *of judgment for every careless word they have spoken. For by your*
> *words you will be acquitted, and by your words you will be*
> *condemned. (Matt 12:36-37)*

This demonstrates the far-reaching implications of the words we speak. No wonder Paul says:

Do not let any unwholesome talk come out of your mouth,
but only what is helpful for building others up according to their
needs, that it may benefit those who listen. (Eph 4:29)

YOU PLACE YOUR LIFE UNDER THE WORDS YOU SPEAK.

James is even stronger in the warnings he gives concerning the use of our tongues. He says that the tongue is a small part of the body, but it makes great boasts. He likens it to the rudder of a ship, only a very small part but it directs the entire course of the ship.

This is the power of the words you speak; they direct the course of your life. **You place your life under the words you speak.** When your words agree with what God says about you and His purpose for your life, then you are on the course that He intends for you. When you disagree with Him, you steer off course.

Consider what a great forest is set on fire by a small spark.
The tongue also is a fire, a world of evil among the parts of the body.
It corrupts the whole person, sets the whole course of his life on fire,
and is itself set on fire by hell. (James 3:5-6)

Does this sound too strong? At Caesarea Philippi, Peter was the first to acknowledge publicly that Jesus was the Christ, the Son of the living God. Now they knew who He was, Jesus chose twice to tell the disciples that He would be rejected and crucified, but that He would be raised from the dead. This did not agree at all with Peter's view of the Messiah. So he takes Jesus to one side and rebukes Him, "Never, Lord!" he said.

> *"This will never happen to you!" (Matt 16:22)*

Jesus turned and said to Peter:

> *Get behind me, Satan! You are a stumbling block to me;*
> *you do not have in mind the things of God, but the things*
> *of men. (Matt 16:23)*

One moment Peter was on course proclaiming Jesus to be who He is. The next he was right off-course, disagreeing with Jesus and speaking against what He said.

This should be a warning to us to agree with what God says about us in His Word. To think we know better than God would be the utmost pride, but would also make us the mouthpiece of Satan, speaking against the truth.

How can we avoid speaking that which is wrong over our lives? Only by believing the truth in our hearts and speaking accordingly.

> *With the tongue we praise our Lord and Father, and*
> *with it we curse men, who have been made in God's likeness.*
> *Out of the same mouth come praise and cursing. My brothers, this*
> *should not be. Can both fresh water and salt water flow from the*
> *same spring? (James 3:9-11)*

Are you going to agree with God, that you are the new person who lives in Christ Jesus, or are you going to see yourself through the eyes of your own flesh and speak sin, fear, failure and negativity over your life?

To confess, or continually express, who you are in Christ is not to be unreal, quite the opposite. This is the reality of how God sees you; you are simply agreeing with Him. You are who He says you are. Paul tells us:

> *Do not conform any longer to the pattern of this world,*
> *but be transformed by the renewing of your mind. Then you will*
> *be able to test and approve what God's will is - his good,*
> *pleasing and perfect will. (Rom 12:2)*

Your mind can only be renewed by a revelation of the truth. If you do not *think* with what is true about yourself, you will not *believe* the truth about yourself; and if you do not believe the truth about yourself, you will not *speak* the truth and this will steer you off course from God's purpose.

> *We demolish arguments and every pretension that sets*
> *itself up against the knowledge of God, and we take captive every*
> *thought to make it obedient to Christ. (2 Cor 10:5)*

This means you have to ignore the negative thoughts about yourself that come from your flesh or from the lying accusations of the enemy. Instead you need to think, believe and speak the truth as God's Word reveals it.

Often you will be tempted to say, *"I can't"*. That may be true of the flesh. The spiritual (or real) truth about you is that you can do all things through Christ who gives you strength.

You can speak of yourself as sick, and that might be true of your physical condition. The spiritual (or real) truth about you is that by the stripes of Jesus you have been healed. How are you going to view your circumstances? You can speak poverty over your life, or you can confess that your God meets your every need through the riches of His glory in Christ Jesus!

You need to learn to speak the truth of who you are in Christ, what you have and what you can do because you are in Him. You can do this in five distinct ways:

SPEAK THE TRUTH TO YOURSELF

You need to hear it continually. David knew the power of doing this. He is speaking to his own soul when he says:

> *Praise the Lord, O my soul; all my inmost being*
> *praise his holy name. Praise the Lord, O my soul and forget*
> *not all his benefits. (Ps 103:1-2)*

He then reminds himself of a series of important truths that he speaks over his life:

- He forgives all my sins
- And heals all my diseases;
- He redeems my life from the pit
- And crowns me with love and compassion
- He satisfies my desires with good things, so that my youth is renewed like the eagle's. *(Ps 103:4-5)*

Because you are in Christ these are truths about you. See yourself as He sees you. Choose to think as He does about your circumstances and keep speaking the truth about yourself to yourself.

SPEAK THE WORD TO GOD

Pray according to His Word. God has revealed His will to us
through His Word. So we know that when we pray according to
what He says and promises to us, that we pray according to His
will!

SPEAK THE WORD TO THE ENEMY

This is how Jesus dealt with the enemy's temptations in the
wilderness: *"It is written …. "*. When speaking of the armour of
God, Paul says we have the *shield of faith* in one hand, with which
we can extinguish all the flaming arrows the enemy fires at us.
These are often in the form of lying accusations or condemning
thoughts.

**Many believers do not realise who is behind their negative
thoughts.** They spend so much time listening to the enemy's lies
they do not hear the voice of the Holy Spirit guiding them into the
truth!

In the other hand you have the *sword of the Spirit,* which is the
Word of God. With the shield of faith you can reject all his lies,
negative thoughts and false condemnation. With the sword of the
Spirit, the Word of God, you cut off all attack. You proclaim boldly
who you are in Christ. The enemy then has to come against the
One in whom you trust, and he flees!

Never argue with the devil or any lying spirits. Dismiss them as
Jesus did: *"Away from me, Satan!"*

SPEAK THE TRUTH TO ONE ANOTHER

One of the ways in which we are to express our love for each other is by speaking the truth in love to one another. In other words we are to remind one another of who we are in Christ:

> *Therefore each of you must put off falsehood and*
> *speak truthfully to his neighbour, for we are all members*
> *of one body. (Eph 4:25)*

When writing to Philemon, Paul speaks a profound truth that I have found so effective in my own experience:

> *I pray that you may be active in sharing your faith,*
> *so that you will have a full understanding of every good*
> *thing we have in Christ. (Philemon 6)*

The more you encourage others with the truth, the more you will be encouraged by it yourself. Because we live surrounded by negative people (who are sometimes Christians) we can speak words of truth that can set them free from the false perceptions they have of themselves and their circumstances! Jesus said:

> *If you hold fast to my teachings, you are really my*
> *disciples. Then you will know the truth, and the truth will*
> *set you free. (John 8:31-32)*

It is so important to take careful note of these words. It is only the truth that will set you free from false perceptions of yourself. In like manner, it is only the truth that will set others free. Prayer, ministry, counselling techniques will not be effective unless you are praying the truth, ministering the truth and counselling people with the truth of who they are in Christ!

You can be a great blessing and encouragement to other believers by reminding them of the truth in your daily conversations whenever you hear them denying the truth by the things they say about themselves.

SPEAK THE TRUTH TO THE WORLD

The world is not waiting with bated breath to hear our latest experience or revelation. People will only come to Christ and become His disciples by hearing and responding to the truth of who God is and what He has done:

> *"The word is near you; it is in your mouth and*
> *in your heart;" that is, the word of faith we are proclaiming:*
> *That if you confess with your mouth, 'Jesus is Lord,' and believe*
> *in your heart that God raised him from the dead,*
> *you will be saved. For it is with your heart that you believe*
> *and are justified, and it is with your mouth that you*
> *confess and are saved. (Rom 10:8-10)*

Note that a person is not saved until he speaks out or confesses the truth to someone else. So we need to be prepared to share the truth with others whenever we have the opportunity to do so:

> *How, then, can they call on the one they have*
> *not believed in? And how can they believe in the one*
> *of whom they have not heard? (Rom 10:14)*

Whenever we speak the truth to others it must always be in love. Remember:

The mouth of the righteous is a fountain of life. (Prov 10:11)

The tongue of the righteous is choice silver. (Prov 10:20)

The lips of the righteous nourish many. (Prov 10:21)